AMBLER, V.

Basketball

This book is due for return on or before the last date shown above but it may be renewed unless required by other readers, by personal application, post, or telephone, quoting this date and the author and title.

BUCKINGHAMSHIRE COUNTY LIBRARY

L 28   **SCHOOL LIBRARY SERVICE**

Competitive Sports Series

BASKETBALL

Vic Ambler

Batsford Academic and Educational
London

© Vic Ambler 1984
First published 1984

Typeset by Tek-Art Ltd, Kent
Printed in Spain by
Grijelmo SA, Bilbao
for the publishers
Batsford Academic and Educational
an imprint of B T Batsford Ltd
4 Fitzhardinge Street
London W1H 0AH

British Library Cataloguing in Publication Data

Ambler, Vic
    Basketball.– (Competitive sports series)
    1. Basketball
    I. Title   II. Series
    796.32'32   GV885

ISBN 0 7134 4423 1

═══════Contents═══════

THE AUTHOR

Vic Ambler is a lecturer in physical education at the University of Exeter. From 1970-81 he was Head Coach of the England Senior Men's Team. In 1976 and 1980 he was on the coaching staff of the Great Britain Olympic Teams.

As visiting coach for the International Olympic Committee to India, Zimbabwe and Saudi Arabia he has experience of the game world wide.

Currently he is Chairman of the EBBA International Committee concerned with the competitive and developmental programmes of all National Teams.

ACKNOWLEDGMENT

Photography by Trevor Pountain, Rod Commons of Washington State University USA.

Drawings by Nigel Weaver, University of Exeter Curriculum Resources Centre.

The author wishes to thank both Trevor Pountain and Nigel Weaver for the illustrations, and Mrs Sue Newall for her extensive secretarial help and guidance.

Introduction

Basketball has been called the international sport of the 1980s. There is hardly a corner of the earth where people of all ages and both sexes have not been attracted by this game of fast movement, amazing accuracy and thrilling, sometimes extraordinary, finishes.

The game is supported by over 160 national federations from the developing countries of Africa to the sophisticated and intensively presented competitions of North America and Europe. In China there are estimated to be around 100 million players – roughly equal to the combined populations of Great Britain and France – playing on dirt courts and in palatial arenas.

International tournaments in Taiwan, Brazil, Tokyo and Belgrade are attended by huge crowds fascinated by the athleticism and skill of mobile giants and quick-moving smaller players. The intricate blend of co-operative and individual skill, flexible enough to accommodate the fireworks of personal duels yet remaining, essentially, a team effort is a unique attraction.

A highly visible sport with the action never obscured, using the largest ball in any team game, the continual thrill of attack and counter-attack appeals to players and spectators who can remain warm, dry and comfortable as they support their chosen team.

Basketball, as we know it today, was born in the United States in 1891 as a recreational activity and quickly spread, culminating in its debut at the Olympic Games in 1936 as a men's sport. The final game was played outside in the rain on tennis courts when the USA defeated Canada by 19-8! The USA continued their Olympic dominance until 1972 when in a dramatic and still controversial finish the USSR stole the game in the last three seconds. The USA reclaimed the Olympic title in 1976 defeating Yugoslavia, another very strong nation who triumphed in Moscow in 1980 in the absence of the USA and Canada. The scene is set for a titanic struggle in Los Angeles in 1984 in the pre-eminent team sport of Olympic competition. The Women's Olympic Competition inaugurated in the 1976 Games has been dominated by the USSR, but as women compete increasingly in sport the skill development in all countries is spectacular and, for example, in Great Britain the number of girls' teams participating in the National Schools Championships has more than doubled in only a few years as the game begins to rival netball both in schools and clubs.

Offensive and defensive reaction

In Great Britain success at international level has been hard to achieve but England in qualifying for the European Finals for both men and women in the early 1980s and winning the Commonwealth Men's Championship in 1983 have pointed to increased hopes in future European, World and Olympic competitions.

The amazing growth and success of the game in Britain with regular television coverage, sell out National League games and Cup Finals, the emergence of many young talented players with a truly nationwide organisation and support places Basketball in the forefront of public interest and future development during the 1980s.

In education, particularly in the secondary schools, but with an increasing number of middle schools, the game is also expanding. Ninety per cent of

An England under 17 player out rebounds the Holland attack

Young players, both boys and girls, show their skill in mini-basketball

secondary schools have provision for Basketball for boys and girls and it is estimated that well over a million pupils are involved. National competitions are held for individual schools and area associations and international teams bringing the great honour of playing for England exist at U15, U17 and U19 levels.

Mini-basketball providing a friendly competitive basis and opportunity for early skills acquisition is growing in the 8-12 age group category and this feature of the game is, with its educational sense and bias, likely to prosper the game even further in future years.

1 The Game

Seeing a game for the first time let alone playing it can be a unique experience. For the football enthusiast used to the odd goal, the continual scoring can stimulate his adrenalin flow and excitement to the point of exhaustion. To the rugby follower the sight of so much skilful ball handling by big men, who he would normally see only rarely with a ball in their hands, is illuminating. All are amazed at the lack of contact and collision in such a speedy game and the absence of bad-tempered flare-ups as five players on each side contest legally for possession on a small court over a 40 minute period of two 20-minute halves aided by two referees who can award fouls for personal or technical offences. Any player recording five such fouls can take no further part in the game and can be substituted.

Each player must therefore learn three basic rules and adopt his skills accordingly.

1   *Avoidance of personal contact* it being the duty of every player to do so. Although there can be incidental contact in a reasonable attempt to play the ball, particularly by a defensive player, the basic principle in skill terms is to stay balanced, upright and in control of one's bodily actions.

2   *No running with the ball.* A player in possession of the ball may only progress with it to the limits of one pace or two foot counts. This rule can be shrouded in complexity but the essential skill development is centred on the two count rhythm in coming to a stop, requiring knee flexion, weight distribution and a relaxed, even 'floppy', receipt of the ball. Receiving the ball whilst standing still results in the permitted movement of only one (usually the front) foot.

3   *A limited dribbling action.* A dribble is a series of bounces of the ball and is often used to get into a shooting position away from defenders, penetrate into a space to give a better pass or move the ball quickly up court. Only one series of bounces is allowed and a player who permits the ball to come to rest in one or both hands has finished the series and cannot then continue to bounce the ball. The dribble is often over-used by inexperienced players and later in this book some advice on skill training is given.

A coaching session in progress

It must be remembered that the context of these rule-related skills is ten players moving with rapidity over a limited space. Indeed the nature of the modern game has increased demands on players and referees but a key figure in Basketball, possibly in a way no other sport has developed, is the teacher-coach.

Not only does the teacher-coach play an integral part by directing the on-court strategy of the team, he is also responsible for helping to develop these rule-related skills in his coaching and training sessions.

The coach can use *time-out* of one minute twice in each half to enable adjustments and developments to be made. He may also coach his team in the game provided he is sitting on the bench and instructs in a reasonable manner. The *half-time* period of ten minutes also allows for him to review tactics and performance. *Substitution* of players who are tired, off form, in foul trouble, or to enable particular skills to be used is also a game strategy and it is usual for all the permitted ten players to get on court in a game. The physical intensity of the game makes substitution acceptable and even necessary. A modern development of full-court continual defence called 'pressure defence' has led to more action and involvement of players who learn to appreciate that defence is as important as scoring baskets.

Anyone can play Basketball. All you need is a ball, small space and some kind of hoop attached to a wall, tree or pole. Desire and willingness to work at developing skills particularly shooting, passing and defence are necessary. Height can give some advantages close to the basket but height alone is no guarantee of success. It has to be backed up with skill and know-how acquired by practice and playing.

The following chapters are designed to increase your appreciation and execution of game skills. The pictures are all in action shots of fine players – study them and prosper!

The game is played outdoors with great skill

≡≡2 Techniques and Skills≡≡

PART 1 Elements

Basketball is a game of momentum. Somebody once said . . . 'when the going gets tough the tough get going'. To avoid a breakdown of skill like missing an easy shot, throwing a bad pass or losing your opposing player whilst on defence under the pressure of a competition game situation, requires intensive training and experience in realistic and game conditions. Indeed a skill is recognised as the execution of technique in some form of game or pressure situation. The increasing involvement of active opposition is necessary for the coach not only to be able to assess skill but also to try to improve it.

The Coach-player interaction

Coaching is about helping players to acquire good habits and avoiding bad ones *but* the co-operation of players is an absolute must. The following analysis holds good:

COACH	PLAYER
Showing the right thing often enough;	Closely observing, listening and acting;
Providing opportunity to practise;	Making time to practise with intensity;
Motivating players in practice;	Having a positive and team attitude;
Helping by correction and advice.	Listening to advice and taking criticism but particularly being enthusiastic.

In practice a player must spend time at the things he isn't good at – concentrate on the hard stuff! 'Extra effort is the difference between an average and a great player.'

When I am asked what attributes go toward making the superior player I always reply:

Attitude   Summarised in enthusiasm; hustle; co-operation with fellow players, coaches, and referees; determination.

Basketball can be a particularly difficult game for some individuals because of the substitution rule. My advice is to play flat out all the time on offence and defence so that you may actually want to be substituted having done a good job and hand over for a spell to a team-mate. If you are unfortunate enough to play little in a particular game then work on those skills which will take you into the starting line up and aid your team

Extra effort!

next time. Always remember 'the amount that can be executed by a *team* is controlled by the weakest man on it'.

Vision   is the second characteristic distinguishing good players. Good passers, shooters and defenders cultivate good vision. A player aims to see as much of the court and players as possible and to free his attention from the ball as soon as he can. This is particularly true in shooting where good shooters see the basket early. In dribbling or passing the head should be up to enable your team-mates to be seen. 'Look outside of yourself' constantly.

Physical characteristics   Although height is a factor, the game provides great opportunity for smaller players and no one should regard height as indispensible. It isn't how tall you are but how you play.

The most important factor is *quickness*. The key to becoming a good player is found here. Be quick, think quick and practise quick are important. The basics of shooting, dribbling, passing and defensive reaction need speed and quickness from the very early stages.

Good physical conditioning is important and various *agility* exercises shown in the appendix are useful.

Jumping ability   is common to basketball players and although the game creates, of necessity, jumping ability, some special training and work is usually merited. Of course in all this must come *stamina*. Basketball requires sustained running but also speed over short distances sometimes in a sideways or even backward direction.

Readers are directed to the appendix and self development plan for some recommended practices but it must again be stressed that Basketball is a total game, and that realistic game situations underpinned by conditioning practices are the most fruitful strategies.

PART 2 Ball Handling

Passing   As long as you have the ball and do not give it away the opposition cannot score. Yet even good teams have problems in retaining the ball against defensive pressure for up to the permitted 30 seconds even if they are not at that time trying to score! It should be easy to do but, because passing and particularly receiving is a neglected skill, teams lose games they should win.

A player in possession of the ball should instantly look to pass to a team-mate in a more advantageous position unless a good scoring opportunity presents itself. In fact the good player has *already* judged his own shooting or passing potential before receipt of the ball but this remains to be learned for the unexceptional beginner which most of us are.

A smaller player showing positioning and agility in order to obtain the ball

Protecting the ball but seeing the action

Although there are certain types of pass (techniques) the skill elements are:

1 To eliminate telegraphing the pass: it is sometimes said that we see but do not look and therefore disguise our intentions from the opposition (and hopefully not from our own team).

2 To use the forearm, wrist and fingers to the degree necessary to make quick and accurate passes. The pass gets its force from this wrist and finger snap and follow through.

3 Aim the pass where it is most advantageous for a team-mate to receive it. It must be remembered that passing is a two-man affair – a passer and a receiver who should receive the ball comfortably and away from the defence. To do this the receiver will usually signal where he needs the ball.

A 'chest' or direct pass

4   Pass through spaces in the defence either created to by-pass a close
    guarding defender by the ball handler using fakes and changing the
    position of the ball or by action to get free by the receiver off the ball.

If a receiver is moving, the passer should lead the receiver or put it
slightly ahead of him.

There are situations in the game when it is more advantageous to lob or
bounce the ball to a receiver but these are specific passes and the
general principle is to use accurate, direct passes.

The two-handed chest pass is a very common pass in the game. It is called
this because it starts as the ball is propelled from the chest or upper trunk
area. It is *not* called a chest pass because it goes to the chest of the receiver,
this is an outmoded concept in these days of close individual defence. The
pass is most used to move the ball easily up the floor or when the ball is
passed around the perimeter of the defensive alignment.

A clear signal is given

Keeping the ball available

The two-handed overhead pass is probably the most used pass in the modern game and is effective in many situations particularly when throwing inside to a tall or post player. It is simply a wristy snap from above, but not behind the head, with a downward action.

The hand-off pass is a crucial skill and is executed when two players are in close proximity to each other and one player moves or cuts by the ball handler who is in a static or post position with his back to the basket. This pass is a must for post players who find space in advance of the defence, meet the ball and then hand off to a cutting player. This movement particularly if linked to a fake underhand pass, a turn to the basket and followed by an overhead pass is a basic attacking move in the game and should be strongly emphasised in early learning and teaching.

The one hand javelin or baseball pass is mainly used following a rebound to get the ball to a player moving down court ahead of the defence. The fingers are spread behind the ball and as release is attempted the hand is 'kept on the ball' to encourage follow through and maximum control. This can be an exhilarating and effective pass if mastered and practised but it can be risky with poor execution.

Javelin pass

Bounce pass

A pass can be bounced to a receiver with one or two hands. The most effective is the one-hand pass preceded by a pivot action to open up the defenders space, but this particular pass can result in lost balls and is *not* considered a basic pass – rather as an alternative in a range of options seeking space in the defence and good safe receipt by a team-mate.

The best practice for passing is in game situations with some conditioned practices and a great deal of coaching as necessary aids. The appendix contains some recommended practices.

Dribbling is an essential skill of the game but should always be selective and never become a habit so that a player on catching the ball automatically bounces it thus reducing his attacking potential.

Keeping the momentum and penetrating the defence

Speed in the dribble

Co-ordinated team play is based upon passing rather than dribbling although there are strategic occasions when this is reversed, ie when a player is unable to pass and must play the ball; when an open route to the basket is available; against a slow moving defender; to eliminate a close-marking defender and open up passing spaces, or to move the ball quickly down floor in a fast attack. But all these are strategic purposes and not an aimless bouncing or an individual ego trip.

There is no doubt that dribbling is an appealing skill and good progress can be made in a short time. Technically the ball is pushed or pressed to the ground and not slapped. To be proficient, a player should learn to dribble with either hand and with the head up seeing the court and particularly the opponent's basket at all times, varying speed and direction. Perhaps the most important concept is to 'move the ball'. The rules prevent the hand from carrying the ball but being able to move it across the body and forward in attack is a valuable skill. The key is to go somewhere quickly. The speed dribble will mean moving the ball ahead, and star dribblers can cover the length of the court in very few bounces – as little as 4 or 5!

Shooting   All other techniques and skills exist to assist or prevent scoring opportunities. Shooting is thus the primary skill of the game and requires a great deal of practice assisted by good models and individual coaching. Let's deal with the *outside shots* (ie more than 6ft from the basket).

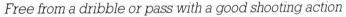

Free from a dribble or pass with a good shooting action

Good co-ordination – waving goodbye in the follow-through

The first thing to remember is that we are talking about one basic action whether shooting from a standing position or off a dribble. The same factors hold good for all shots in the range of the individual. If a player is outside his range and straining then he is currently not shooting the ball but throwing it. Clearly strength, or more correctly, co-ordination is the crucial factor. A smooth, continuous economical effort is what is required.

Target There is continual discussion on the aiming point, whether it is to be the front or back or middle of the rim. My view is that the shooter should at least try to visualise the middle but this factor is less important than seeing the basket early and maintaining constant vision and focus until the shot is completed. It is true that we aim to shoot over the front rim and not the back one! All shots should be aimed straight into the basket rather than off the backboard to retain the one shot idea and not to have several shots from different positions.

Balance The co-ordination required for good shooting is a summation of continuous action generated by the legs, trunk, arms, hand and fingers. The ball is held at chest level, feet parallel, knees bent, shoulders square to the basket, both hands relaxed on the sides of the ball.

Getting into a good shooting position. Balanced, knees flexed, eyes on the basket

Release   The ball is lifted in a continuous action to above and slightly in front of the head, as the legs stretch and push upwards. The shooting hand moves under the ball, the other hand remaining on the side. The ball is kept in the midline of the body. Delivery is made with a stretching action and follow through to impart some back spin. We talk about 'waving good-bye' to the ball. The trajectory is about 60°. Good co-ordination will result in the shooter finishing on the toes or even leaving the floor slightly. As with all shots concentration and confidence are important elements.

Common faults
  – checking the ball on the upward motion
  – dropping the ball back on the wrist when overhead
  – poking the shoulder forward and imparting bias
  – flicking the ball away and not keeping the hand on the ball long enough
  – trying to increase power and range too early and executing a
        jump/throw
  – not keeping a vertical axis – good shooters don't move forward
  – not arching the ball enough or too much.

The one hand shot from stationary and dribbling positions is the foundation of shooting and worth the time, effort and patience required.

The jump shot.   There are some minor variations in technique depending on the height of players and distance from the basket but the jump shot is very similar to the one-hand set shot except that the player may consciously leave the floor and it is often shot from a moving, ie a dribbling, situations.

It is however a fallacy to encourage players to jump over defenders. The aim of successful shot is to get free and in space not to shoot the risky closely-guarded shot.

A scoring shot

30

A scoring lay-up shot. Eyes on the backboard, wrist and finger delivery

The dribble is intended to take the shooter clear of the defender, to come to a two foot, feet parallel, position and to shoot almost exactly the same as before.

Some coaches use a dribble, dip, square, shoot emphasis which is effective. It is of course advantageous to shoot off a dribble going either way with left and right hand dribbles.

The modern shot needs to be a quick one as the player receives a good pass already squared off to the basket or creates the opportunity off the dribble.

The inside shots. *The major variations are the front, sideways and reverse or hook shots. The term lay-up shot is often used to describe some of these* because the ball is 'laid up' on to the backboard but, as we shall see, there are occasions when the shot is aimed directly into the basket. It is desirable to use either hand to give more options. *The one-hand lay-up shot is* performed at different speeds, from different angles and under varying degrees of defensive pressure.

(a) An *undefended shot* against a weak or slow back defence is the simplest
and probably earliest shot to learn. The shot is made from a pass or
dribble using an overhand stretching delivery off the backboard. Most
players shoot a right handed shot by coming off the left foot to balance the
body and approach at an angle of about 45°.

Key factors are to get high by jump and reach and to see the basket early
by keeping the head up. Young players often find difficulty because they
have their head down and do not see the basket early, thus rushing the
shot. Using the board is preferable to a direct shot here.

(b) A *lay-up shot* may be used against a close- marking defender. This shot
is sometimes called a *reverse lay up* which, although spectacular, is also
a good scoring weapon. It also forms a good basis for developing the

15 moves inside the defence in a slide shot   *A good hook-shot action*

hook shot later. The ball is reversed off the board over the inside shoulder, ie the one nearest the backboard.

(c) A *slide shot* is effective because it requires less space and affords good protection against a defender. To execute this shot a sideways dribble parallel to the baseline, with a last high bounce to spring upward, is often used. On delivery the shoulders are square to the baseline, the ball is released high and late with one hand cutting down the area of a defender's interception. This shot is very valuable for the bigger players inside and deserves to be learned and coached more often.

The hook shots are a development of reverse shots in that they are initiated with the back of the shooter to the basket. Since this a common position on receiving the ball, particularly for taller players, it is an important shot to learn and is difficult to defend.

The player steps with the non-pivot foot towards or lateral to the basket and delivers the ball with the hand and arm opposite that leg. The head turns to locate the basket early, rotating the body and using a short hooking action to put the ball directly into the ring. A variation of the direct hook is to dribble across the key and put the ball over the front edge of the ring. This shot can be particularly effective for quick forwards.

PART 3 Defensive techniques

It is not possible to consider individual techniques without considering the defensive strategy of teams. one- and two-man bands can exist, defence requires a whole team and integrated effort. Young players find defensive techniques difficult and unrewarding with sometimes little recognition by coaches and spectators of their value. This is a situation which is changing, and successful coaches and teams are, these days, defensively minded.

The primary team defence is in a man-for-man assignment, developments of this initial defence can be made including zone defences but essentially and initially the man-for-man responsibility is vital to skill development and eventual strategic efficiency. Team defence is therefore is therefore based on good individual defence and the following aspects are important:

1   See man and ball
Vision is just as important on defence as on offence. Since man for man defence reacts to ball *and* player movement it is essential that the defender retains vision of both and adjusts his position to maintain this situation. However, there are fleeting situations in which one may be lost – if this occurs keep the offensive man in sight hoping to stop an effective pass getting to him.

2   Move the feet when defending a dribbler
To do this a defender should move in a sideways position which is termed a *shuffle* maintaining a legal defensive position throughout. A legal position is

Defender sees man and ball

achieved with both feet on the ground facing the dribbler and attempting to gain the first position denying an open route to the basket. This continual 'push and pull' pattern of leg movements is demanding but it cannot be too strongly emphasised, and the legs must do the work. Any attempt to use the arms to knock the ball away will, particularly with younger players, result in unbalancing, break in rhythm and possible fouls.

3 *Use the hands to discourage an effective pass or shot*
A good defender is always close to his man when he has the ball. He must be instantly ready to react to the triple threat of shooting, dribbling or passing, and preferably in that order.

(a) Against a possible shot the defender will get very close with one hand up to deter or block the shot. In a good offence this can be a difficult assignment but there is no alternative – he must get there!

(b) The dribbler is covered as above.

(c) Close pressure on a passer can result in a held ball and therefore a jump ball situation and potential re-possession. Pressure can also result in a weak or strained pass particularly when the defender's team-mates are covering their men and easy passing targets cannot be seen. The defender with quick hands is invaluable to his team.

Defender establishing position against the dribble

Pressure on the ball handler, ready to defend pass or dribble

4   Block out on rebound situations

It is fair assumption that an offensive team will miss more shots than they make, particularly from outside. This holds good even more with beginner and inexperienced players. The rebounding situations off the ring or board are therefore a key factor in possession and can determine control and the result of the game.

The defensive players close to the basket *must* obtain a position in the path of their offensive players, stay in the inside position and gauge the time to go to the backboard and possibly get the ball by getting higer and wider than the opposition.

Whites get the inside position and 55 gets high and wide

A helping defence by England

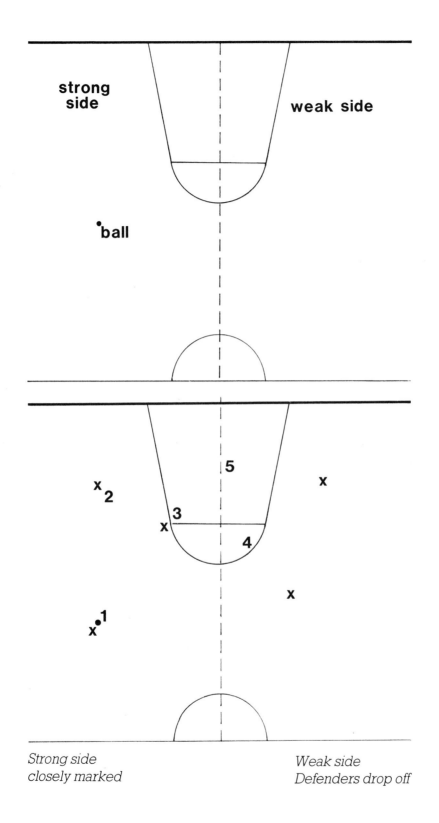

strong side

weak side

ball

5

x 2

3

x

x

4

x

x 1

Strong side
closely marked

Weak side
Defenders drop off

Defensive players at a greater distance may obtain the inside position depending upon the team strategy. When in doubt as to the situation and coach instructions, the rule is to get inside and anticipate a long rebound.

Good positioning can compensate for a lack of jumping ability but clearly both are important. A good jump at the wrong time may produce nothing and the co-ordination of positioning, timing and jumping is a complex skill which needs much practise and not a little ability. Most practices (see appendix) are conducted therefore in realistic and competitive situations.

5 Give help to team-mates

This is particularly relevant on an offensive dribble-penetration. The continuum from individual to co-ordinated defensive play is represented here. The defence must become sensitive to an imaginary line drawn down the middle of the court dividing it into a *strong* or ballside defence and a *weak* or helpside defence on the attacking side of the court.

The ballside players must play close to their opposition with the player defending the immediate ball handler close and tough as previously described: his immediate colleagues may be slightly off their men but must be able to recover within one pass.

On the help side a player may drop off or sag off his man even further toward the mid line ensuring defence in depth against a dribbler able to beat his initial defence or to obtain superior rebound position.

When the ball changes sides the defence will adjust their positions accordingly. The strength of this particular defence in depth is to allow help on a good dribbler and to defend the high scoring area with extra players.

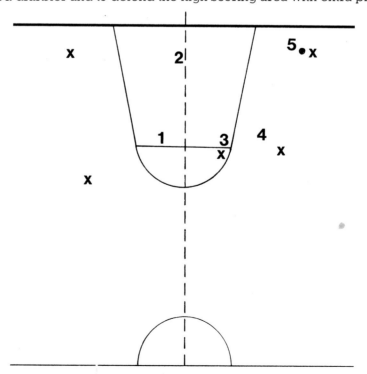

Change of ball position creates change in defensive positions

The defensive line is established and ready to help

6   *Adjust position on change of possession*

(a) From attack to defence. Particularly when a shot is scored and sometimes when it misses a quick change is required. This transition game is necessary to stop the opponents fast breaking or attack. The defensive players must sprint back to the defending area (the attacking third) although there are often situations when stopping an early pass might be of major importance. The coach will usually give guidance on this tactic. The defence must see the ball as ever and pick up their opponent as quickly as possible. A player in the last line of defence may need to temporarily *switch* to an early runner and a communication between players is important. This is a difficult phase and can lead to confusion and the necessity to get back to the basket area and then pick up the opponent vocally (I've got 12!) will be obvious.

(b) From defence to attack. This quick transition is dealt with under *Team offence.*

A zone defence is sometimes used by teams and it has some merit but it cannot be too strongly emphasised that zones are complex and are a development of man-for-man defence not a substitute for it. In reality a zone defence in operation is a sagging defence with continual switching of players. Defenders who are unable to perform the basics and to communicate and move effectively will find the confusion of roles disadvantageous. Zones are not suitable for beginners and young players and should not be employed with these groups.

Following the development of man-for-man skills a team may elect to defend outside the attacking third of the court. They may extend the active defence to half-way, two-thirds or even full court. These are usually termed *pressure defences.* They are difficult and demanding to play but have several advantages. Not least they tend to emphasise defence and make substitution both desirable and necessary, keeping a full team happier.

Against poor passing and dribbling teams they take the initiative and can give a strong psychological boost. Since a team must attempt a shot within 30 seconds and move out of their half in 10 seconds they can, properly applied, put time pressure and produce a hurried shot by the opposition.

A pressure defence accentuates the appreciation of the mid-line principle and increases the need for helping. It may also team or double up by placing two players in a trapping situation on a ball handler.

A pressure defence will expose defensive weakness but it can be a very effective weapon with well prepared teams but be careful not to foul!

England try to pressure the ball

3 Team Attack

The fast break

Although there are times when a team will wish to slow down, the fast break is normally the initial attack. The phases are:

(a) Obtaining rebound possession and getting away a quick pass to a free and preferably moving player. The receiver will often be at the side

The rebound is taken and 12 moves clear on to attack

14 leads the fast break with 50 and 4 moving into supporting positions

where the area is least crowded but, under some conditions, a pass to a player moving down court can be used. This longer pass will often need to be a javelin pass.

(b) Advancing the ball up court. Passing ahead to a free player or dribbling at speed if no player is ahead to keep the momentum going.

Running in support by at least two leading players to ensure width in attack.

(c) Getting in position to score. A team attack will involve getting the ball to the opponents free throw line and having players on either side of the court running hard for a scoring pass.

The passing game

The objective of a team is to achieve a high-percentage shot from a more advantageous position. The pass is the primary means of doing this and the dribble a secondary means. This is particularly true in the initial stages of player and team development where over-emphasis on strictly ordered and precision play demands much more training time and stifles individual skill development. Even experienced league players have problems in remembering controlled play and, although they certainly have a place, it is likely that, like zone defences, they are a development rather than substitution of good passing and moving skills.

Alignment
Even in the passing game an initial alignment of starting positions is necessary. Most coaches designate 2 *guards*, 2 *forwards* and 1 *centre* although this could be changed, eg to have 1 guard, 2 forwards, 2 centres given certain skills and height patterns.

Guards are usually more proficient ball handlers, particularly in dribbling and passing, and in most cases are shorter, possibly quicker, players.

Forwards need to be all-round players of mid height and able to possess all-round shooting skills both close in and outside as well as rebounding abilities.

Centres are usually the taller players, good inside shooters, rebounders and able to distribute the ball effectively particularly with their back to the basket.

A stating alignment might thus be as shown.

Spacing   The attack seeks to spread the defence and therefore distances of about 12-15 ft (3.5-4.5 m) are generally kept. There will be a good deal of necessary movement but staying wide before moving, *having looked first*, will be beneficial. Players often move too early and encouragement to slow down but go hard on the eventual move will be necessary. The important thing to remember is that when you have the ball you are in charge of things!

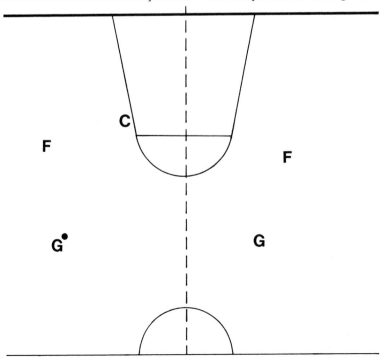

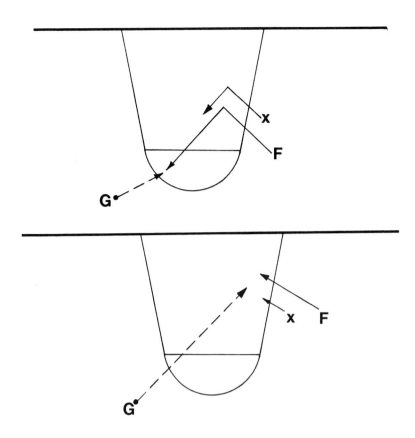

Movement

(a) A closely marked player without the ball is expected to try to free himself. The simpler way to do this is to move toward the basket initiating a reaction by the defender. The offensive player can then turn back toward the ball, presenting a good target to the passer. Of course, if the defender is slow or does not react (this is sometimes the case of the defender who is watching the ball exclusively), the offensive man can keep going and pick up a pass near the basket. The first movement is called a 'V' cut and the second a 'backdoor' move.

(b) (i) A player receiving the ball should firstly assess his opportunity for a good shot (it helps, remember, if he can pre-estimate this ahead of time, for example the closer he is to the basket the more likely it will be).

    (ii) He should then look for a return pass to the player who passed to him.

    (iii) If this option is not taken he looks to any other player getting free.

    (iv) If no one is free he *may* look to dribble and penetrate the defence.

A player who has therefore passed the ball should;

(a) Move to the basket for a return pass – he should never stand still.

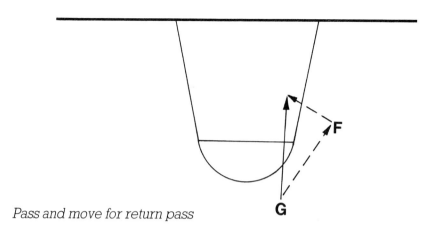

Pass and move for return pass

(b) He may wait near the basket, but outside the restricted area, for up to 3 seconds after which, if he does not receive a pass, he will move away from the ball creating space for another player. A position close to the basket is particularly effective for the taller player who may get a good shot.

The emphasis is on change of direction, change of speed and seeing the entire attacking area.

As the pattern develops the coach may suggest alternatives and developments.

Development

(a) Players are reminded, having immediately passed, that they can move to the basket INSIDE, OUTSIDE and AROUND the defender.

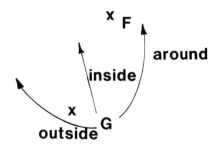

Moving around creates a 'screen' situation as the receiving player pivots away from the basket and gives a hand-off pass. A screen is a legal obstruction and defensive players get lost in the traffic.

(b) A player who can 'flash' from the weakside toward the ball, usually coming from the baseline to the top of the key area, is in a particularly good position. This action is called *posting*.

50

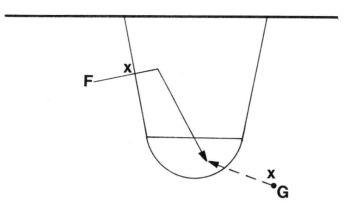

This attacking position in the centre of the court gives the offence more options and causes problems for the defence in identifying the strong and weak sides and adjusting accordingly.

Screening

(c) Screening. A player can be instructed to screen away from the ball. This is the setting of a legal obstruction to a team-mate's defensive player so that the team-mate can lose his defender and go to the basket.

This type of mobile (sometimes called *motion attack*) is ideal for young players and forms an excellent basis for development. It puts the coach in the role of observer/adviser and most modern coaches agree that it improves coaching techniques and brings all players into the attacking game. There are sophisticated developments which can be used but they are beyond the scope of this particular book.

Against zone defences

It may be that despite our concentration on man-for-man defence the team will come up against a zone. It will be found that the passing game will work well against this type of defence, particularly if the ball is passed more quickly, the cutting players are balanced and prepared for a quick shot and you add one more ingredient, that of rotation. In rotation which is essentially a three-man series the pass, move and return pass is retained, but the third player off the ball will fill the space created by the cutter coming in to a shooting position.

This is effective because defenders, instead of marking players directly, will retain a floor position and we are effectively giving the initial defender two attacking players to defend in the same space. This principle can later be extended but coaches expecting zone defences can emphasise this aspect in early teaching.

A further point on the passing game is how it forms a blueprint for not only the teaching of passing in its initial stages but will also indicate to the observant coach the defensive techniques required. In essence it can provide the basis for a 'scheme of work' for teacher-coaches. Defence will improve in squad sessions through playing against this offence.

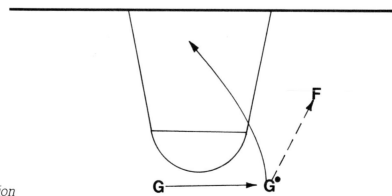

Rotation

Dribbling is thus limited, even initially, to
(a) improving passing angles
(b) getting out of trouble
(c) driving through gaps usually to the basket. A useful initiation is to limit a dribble to 2 or 3 bounces at maximum.

4 Self-Development Plan for Young Players

Your teacher or coach can give you help and instruction but to be a good player you need to work on your own as well. Here are some ideas to help you. *Keep a chart of your improvement.*

Passing

1   Use a wall to practise your passes. A chest pass or overhead pass is used for repetition passing at about 8-10 feet. How many passes can you make in 30 seconds? This will strengthen your passing action.

2   Pass for accuracy. Mark a target on a wall. See how far you can pass accurately using chest, overhead *and* javelin pass.

Dribbling

1   Put five chairs and markers at about two-metre intervals. How many chairs can you complete in 30 seconds in a weaving dribble?

2   Dribble across the centre circle and back changing hands each time. How many trips in 30 seconds?

Lay-up shots

1   Try the skills previously described.

2   How many baskets can you score in 30 seconds continuous shooting changing sides each time you score?

3   Shoot 50 lay-ups in 5 minutes going back outside the key each time before the next shot.

Outside shots

1   Shoot 25 in five minutes from outside the key. Get the ball before it touches the floor, shoot from outside again.

2   Shoot continuous scoring shots from the free throw line – what is your record for continuous scoring shots?

3   Mark your favourite shooting spot. Get someone to pass to you as you move into that spot from at least two strides away. What is
(i) Your record of continuous successful shots?
(ii) your best score out of 10?

4   Dribble around two obstacles to your favourite spot covering at least 10 feet. Shoot a jump shot off the dribble.
What is your record and best score out of 10?

Defensive slides

Shuffle across the centre circle and back. Your outside foot must be outside the circle on each trip. Maintain a front facing position with no crossing of feet and knees bent.

How many trips in 30 seconds?

Run the lines

Start under the basket. Run to near foul line and back, run to half-way and back, run to far foul line and back, run to far base line and back *all* continuously. You have just run about 130 metres.

What is your time?

Rebound control

Tap the ball against the backboard so that it strikes the board above the level of the ring. (For younger players anywhere on the board will do.)

What is your score of taps in 30 seconds?

Can you do it continuously? No stopping?

Can you use either hand?

Appendix

Drills and Practices

In addition to the self-development plan and the full team practices
previously indicated some worthwhile practices and drills follow. Some are
game form practices and can be used with a group of players such as a school
class.

Passing
1 Initially in pairs without opposition, pass and move for return pass using
  legal stop. Include meeting the ball ie moving toward the pass and use
  hand off pass to return.
2 2 v 1 in grids with defender
  (a) Closely guarding ball handler who creates passing space by faking
      and pivoting.
  (b) Closely guarding the receiver so that he works to get free and
      establish a good receiving position meeting the ball signalling and
      catching with two hands.
3 2 v 2 developed to 3 v 3 team passing to achieve a specified number of
  passes. Re-start with jump ball. Use all passes including the hand off.
4 4 v 4 Shell drill. Offensive players in a square formation can move two
  paces in any direction against a closely guarding defence. Get free and
  establish position. Passers must direct the ball away from the defence.
5 Rotation drill in 3s and 4s. Pass move and player off ball fills the space.
  See chapter 3: *Team Attack.*

organisation may require some general practices such as:
(a)   Pass and move in circles of five or six players. No passes to adjacent
      players. Passer takes place of person to whom he passed.
  (b) As above with one or two defenders who try to touch the ball. A poor
      (touched) pass puts the passer in the middle.
  (c) Players in a square. Pass down sides of square and move to middle to
      receive return pass. Pass back to same player and join end of the line.

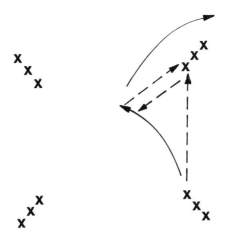

Stretching out the distance and using a javelin pass can be introduced with this drill.

Fast break – developed from passing on the move.
1   Full court posts.

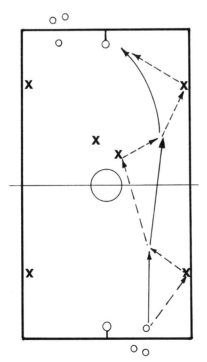

2   Three-man full court passing.
     (a) Rebounder passes to player on side and follows his pass to that side of the court. First receiver passes to a second receiver at mid court and ahead of him following his pass and going behind the receiver to the far side.

57

(b) Continuing this in sequence so that a passer moves behind the man he passes to and goes to the outside. Receivers get ahead of the ball off the ball and come to the middle from the side.
This is called a *weave* and is a basic practice.

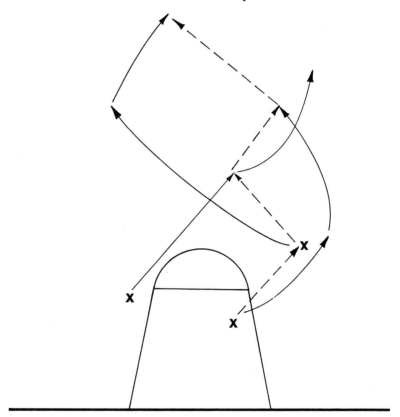

(c) An addition to this is for the ball handler to dribble if no one is ahead of him but to pass as soon as a receiver is available. Alternatively he can dribble to the free throw line to seek a scoring pass or shot.

3 Addition of defence by either the coach or additional players in a 3 v 1 or 3 v 2 situation will increase the options and improve skill.

4 3 v 2 to 2 v 1.
Three players attack two to score. On a score or interception the two defensive players become the attack against a designated defender from the initial three. To continue three new attackers go against two from the other end.

5 Continuous 3 v 3.

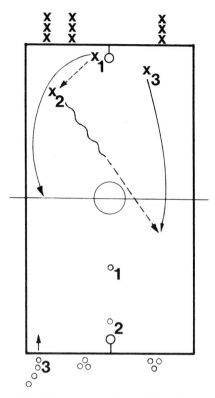

Dribbling – progress to looking at coach and basket.

1   Free dribbling changing speed and direction stopping legally off a fast dribble.
2   Changing hands, moving the ball across the body – a line may be useful as an aid making the ball bounce either side of the line.
3   Avoiding other dribblers in confined space.
4   1 v 1 keep dribbling ball against legal defence in confined space.
5   Speed dribble across spaces, around obstacles and against two or three lined up defenders each of whom charges the ball in half or one third court.
    Time and team competitions can be introduced.
6   Full court 1 v 1. The dribbler must change complete direction at least once in each half and go to score against a moving defender. (Also a good defensive drill)
7   How many dribbles to achieve a lay-up shot receiving the ball initially at the free throw line extended.

Shooting

Inside shots. (see also chapter 4 *Self-development Plan*)
Practices are used from each side and with each hand.
1   Pass and move for return pass and shoot
    (a) from player at side of court giving return pass

(b) from a post player giving a hand off return pass

(c) from a post player who allows the passer to go by to the basket and gives him an overhead pass.

The position on receipt of the ball and position of the defender (when added) will dictate the shot used and whether a dribble is necessary. Speed is essential to introduce in the non defended phase even if there is an occasional missed shot.

2   Defender chasing

The ball passer gives the ball to a player about 6 ft ahead of him and then chases him to try to legally defend the shot.

3   1 on 1

Ball handler fakes and attempts to dribble by the defender who gauges his defence to put degrees of pressure on the shot. Attacking player shoots lay-up reverse or slide shot first to coach request and then to his perceived option.

Outside shots

The emphasis is getting into space and shooting quickly with good form.

1   Grooving

The player is passed balls continuously to shoot the same shot repetitively. An organisation of balls and feeders is necessary.

2   Moving into a shooting position square to the basket receiving 10 passes from under the basket. Move to right and left alternatively.

3   Dribbling into a shooting position going right and left. Players try to cut down the setting up dribble and to go somewhere. A development is to pass off to another shooter having drawn the defence to the possible shot.

4   Pass to post player receiving hand off or overhead pass and shoot with minimum dribbling.

5   Rotation drill is three. Taking the place of the initial ball handler who goes to the basket. Arrive for pass in a shooting position.

6   11 or 21 up. Two teams at each basket. Receiver shoots from free throw line, recovers the ball whether successful or not, passes to passing line and joins the end of it. Change sides after a team reaches the required score. Calling out successful baskets puts pressure on the opposition.

7   Corner shooting competition

Players in pairs, one passer and one shooter. Shoot within designated range from corner area. A shot scored and shooter must change sides otherwise he may stay in same spot. Passer must retrieve ball and feed shooter. Change over on five successful shots. Each pair is required to get 10 scores and win the pair's competition.

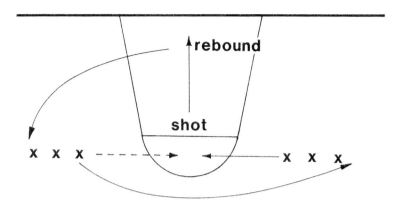

Defensive drills – encouraging agility and general defensive movement.
1   Loose ball 1 v 1. As previous section but ball can be thrown down middle.
    Play 1 on 1 on possession as before.
2   Drive to continuous 1 on 1. Defensive player gives ball to attacker on
    basket side of him and about 2 metres ahead. Defender tries to establish
    position and defend shot. Game continues on a score until one player
    scores three baskets.
3   Bump drill. Offensive dribbler defended in legal shuffle. Dribbler bumps
    (gently) the defender in chest and continues dribble.
4   2 v 2 post defence. Offensive pair use hand off pass to attack basket. Rear
    defender (or post player) switches to driver whilst other defender
    switches to post player.
5   3 v 3 sliding drill. Three offensive players dribble and turn back to basket
    to give hand off pass to cutting player. Defenders stay with their own man
    and 'slide' through the defence.
6   2 on 2 jump switch. Offensive dribbler goes around his defender. Second
    defender 'jumps' in legal defensive position to contain dribbler and make
    him stop. First defender picks up loose man.
7   Press circles. Circle of six to eight players with two or three defenders in
    circle. Outside players may not pass to player on either side. One
    defender must closely defend player in possession and try to force a poor
    pass. Other defenders try to intercept ball. Change over frequently.

General agility and conditioning

1   *Bench jumps.* A normal gymnasium bench can be used.
     (a) Using both feet jump over and back as quickly as possible for 30
         seconds initially building up to one minute. An immediate rebound or
         'touch and go' principle is used.
     (b) Step over bench with one foot followed by the other then back over
         one foot at a time. Build up time factor.
     (c) Stand astride bench and jump both feet to stand on bench.
     (d) Stand sideways to bench. Step sideways with one foot then the other
         to stand on bench and down one foot at a time to far side. Repeat to
         come back and start.
     (Similar jumps using an old car tyre can also be used)

2   *Rope Jumping* (skipping)
     (a) Full speed both feet – object is to do one minute with no misses.
     (b) Left foot hop for 30 seconds followed by right foot for 30 seconds.

3   *Transition drills* using time and speed increases.
     (a) Keeping low move backward from baseline to free throw line and
         forward to baseline again.
     (b) Defensive shuffle around free throw area square turning at each
         corner and reversing direction from starting point.
     (c) Run the lines (see chapter 4: *Self-development plan*).

4   *Rebounding*
     (a) Continuous taps above ring level on board, 30 secs and maximum.
     (b) Continuous taps with partner across the board over the ring.
     (c) Continuous two hand ring touches.

5   *Loose ball* 1 v 1. Coach rolls out a ball to top of key from baseline. Two
     competing players outside key try to get the ball and then play 1 on 1 full
     court.

Additional reading

Available from the English Basketball Association or good bookshops

Basketball Concepts and Techniques, Cousy and Power, Allyn and Bacon, 2nd edition 1970
  A comprehensive American book for coaches

Basketball: Know the Game, E P Sport, 1978

Basketball, Coleman and Ray, E P Sport, 1976
  Popular English book – well illustrated, covers individual and team skills

Basketball – Basics for Coach and Player, Vic Ambler, Faber, 1979
  Basics for coaches, teachers and players from one of England's top international coaches

Basketball: Multiple Offense and Defense, Dean Smith, Prentice-Hall, 1982
  The University of North Carolina were the USA's Champion College in 1981/82 and Dean Smith has led them for many years as Head Coach

Winning Basketball Systems, Jerry Tarkanian, Allyn and Bacon, 1981
  The book is perfect for all levels of coaching. Offers in-depth examinations of all the major successful systems of basketball play. Tarkanian is coach to The University of Nevada, Las Vegas

Basketball Fundamentals – Teaching Techniques for Winning, Jack Lehane, Allyn and Bacon, 1980

Dan Lloyd's Book of Basketball, Pelham, 1983
  Multi-capped Great Britain and England forward Dan Lloyd looks at the English scene and gives help and advice for all. Interesting reading

Also available from the EBBA, Calomax House, Leeds 9, are scorepads, yearbooks, wallcharts, and other general information.

Index